The Purrfect Companion

Learning About Life From Our Feline Friends

H. NORMAN WRIGHT

paintings by SUEELLEN ROSS

HARVEST HOUSE PUBLISHERS

Eugene, Oregon

Sueellen Ross

H. Norman Wright,
proud owner of Mozart, a
British Shorthair kitten, is also
the author of more than 60
books on communication,
marriage, and family. He and
his wife, Joyce, have a married
daughter, Sheryl, and a son,
Matthew, now deceased.

Sueellen Ross is a nationally
known artist whose bestselling
cat calendar with Amcal has
been in print since 1997. Her
art masterfully captures the true
personality of cats and emulates
her love for the feline population.
She and her husband live
in Seattle.

The Purrfect Companion
Text Copyright © 2001 by H. Norman Wright
Published by Harvest House Publishers
Eugene, Oregon 97402

Wright, H. Norman.
    The purrfect companion/ H. Norman Wright ; paintings by Sueeleen Ross.
       p. cm.
    ISBN: 0-7369-0425-5
       1.Cats–Miscellanea. 2.Cats–Quotations, maxims, etc. I.Ross, Sueellen, 1941- II.
    Title.
SF445.5 .W75 2001
636.8'0887–dc21   00-059756

Artwork is reproduced under license from Mill Pond Licensing and may not be reproduced without permission.
For information regarding art prints by Sueellen Ross, please contact:

    Mill Pond Press
    310 Center Court
    Venice, FL 34292
    800.237.2233

Design and production by Koechel Peterson and Associates, Minneapolis, Minnesota

Harvest House Publishers has made every effort to trace the ownership of all poems and quotes. In the event
of a question arising from the use of a poem or quote, we regret any error made and will be pleased to make
the necessary correction on future editions of this book.

Answers to quiz in "Feline Fun" (p. 20):

1) cat nap	7) cat's pajamas or cat's meow	12) catnip
2) cat's cradle	8) cat and mouse	13) catfish
3) catwalk	9) CAT scan	14) cool cat
4) cat burglar	10) cat tails	15) catbird seat
5) cat has your tongue	11) cat's eye	
6) the cat that swallowed the canary		

Printed in Hong Kong

01 02 03 04 05 06 07 08 09 10 / NG / 10 9 8 7 6 5 4 3 2

CONTENTS

How Cats Enrich Our Lives

Can you imagine your life without a cat? For a dedicated cat lover, that's not a pleasant thought. True, cats require time, patience, energy, and understanding of their unique nature, but they're worth it. And when you have a cat, it's not who owns who, it's a relationship. When your life has been touched by a cat, you're never the same. Someone once said an ordinary cat can make an ordinary life extraordinary. That's so true. A cat can bring out the laughter from your heart just when you thought you'd never hear that sound again. Lonely? Not when there's a cat in your life. Their companionship is right under your feet (if you have a cat, you know what I mean).

In ancient times, cats were worshiped as gods; they have never forgotten this.

ANONYMOUS

SueellenRoss

Kittens remind you that life is to be experienced to the fullest and enjoyed to the utmost. Their curiosity about everything reminds you to stop and notice what you've been ignoring. Perhaps they teach us to get as excited about life as they do about a piece of string.

You don't always have to carry on a conversation with your cat. A silent language exists between the two of you. You just have to listen for it.

A cat reminds you of the pleasure of a full stomach, the delights of butterflies in the garden, the warmth of the sun on your back, and the essence of just being still.

Oh, sure, cats have an independent streak (and it's most of the time). Your cat will teach you that you cannot control everything in life. He won't come running the minute you call him, but leave a message and he'll get back to you at his convenience (translated: when he's hungry or wants to be petted).

Cats are magicians. They know when you're going to take them to the vet or give them medicine. They disappear. But the minute your hand brushes the can opener, guess who appears with a "Yo. What's for dinner?" They're great at anticipating what you're going to do next. You head for your favorite chair and guess who beats you to the seat?

What does your cat do for you? Maybe he teaches you about life, such as: always explore unconventional uses for everyday items; it's best to lick your wounds in private; it's easier to make friends if you keep your claws to yourself; and appreciate what time you have together. If you want to learn how to grow old gracefully, just watch your cat.

God created all creatures, large and small, including cats. Where would we be without them?

A dog, quick as a rowboat
to your side, is your best
friend in a minute. A cat,
turning slowly like the
great ocean liner, is your
friend for life.

ANONYMOUS

CHAPTER ONE

Do You Remember...?

Remember your first cat? I remember mine. In fact, I have a picture of me as a four-year-old boy sitting on the back step of our house with a basket of kittens on my lap. The year was 1941. You can see the delighted expression on my face as the kittens and I look at one another. It was a typical litter that included two white, one tortoise shell, and one that defied description.

Those four (and their mother) were my glorious introduction to the world of cats. Each one had its own personality as well as habits. Some of them were sane while others seemed a bit peculiar. Each lived in a world of its own and at times even invited me into that world.

This litter provided me with what every child wants—entertainment. Kittens entertained them

selves but to add to their antics, all you had to do was take a cardboard box, cut in doors and windows, and set it down. As soon as the box was placed on the floor, they claimed it as their playhouse.

Like people, kittens make mistakes and can end up in trouble. A stocky, pure white one didn't know the meaning of the word *boundaries*. It's not that she was dysfunctional, just overly inquisitive.

One day it happened. It was a simple formula. Just take one overly curious kitten, one old-fashioned pint-glass mason jar with a bit of tasty substance inside, and you have a cat running around the yard with its head stuck inside the jar. She was so frantic she never saw the side of the house until she ran into it head on! Well, do you remember the old soap commercial "ring around the collar"? The glass had shattered leaving the kitten without a scratch, but now she had a jagged glass-jar collar. After composing ourselves from our laughing fits, my mother and I decided to rescue her. With a hammer we took care of the collar—miraculously without cutting the cat or ourselves!

Then there were the persistent cats (aren't they all?). My dad had his own room where he would sit, read, and smoke his White Owl cigar in the evening. The French doors leading to this room were glass so you could see in and out. Boots, a big orange male cat with white feet, decided that doors were meant to be opened. Dad would get comfortable and begin reading his Western

Sueellen Ross

novel. After a while Boots would come into the house, eat, and then wander through each room to see where the action was. He would come to Dad's door and probably think, "Huh, he's in there. I'm out here. That's just not going to work." So he would stand on his hind paws and begin scratching on the window.

Boots knew the word *persistent*. It was predictable what would eventually unfold during the nightly ritual. First, Dad would ignore the sound. (Have you ever tried to ignore a persistent cat? Were you *ever* successful? If so, you're the first.) Then Dad would yell at him (the doors did a good job muffling the sound.) Next, he'd toss a book at the door to scare Boots away. Boots would stop, look through the door, and think, "Well, there's the nightly book toss. Now let's get on with it." He would stand again with an intensified effort, and before long Dad would get up, open the door, let him in, and say a few

uncomplimentary remarks to the cat. Boots never stayed long. He'd look around, sniff, look at Dad with an air of, "Yuk, this place smells worse than my cat box," and walk out the door. Truthfully, I don't think Dad really minded.

Feline Frenzy

Our son, Matthew, was a profoundly mentally retarded boy who died at 22. When he lived at home, cats were a part of his life. I don't know how much of his life's surroundings ever registered with him because he was less than a two-year-old intelligence-wise, but one day Matthew had a significant encounter with our cat, Sylvester.

The cat was asleep in my easy chair with his blue-gray tail draped over the side of the chair. It seemed to have a sign on it that said, "Pull me." I'll never know what was going through Matthew's mind when he walked in, but he saw Sylvester sleeping and grabbed his tail with a vice-like grip.

Have you ever seen a cat wake up—in shock? Have you ever seen a cat's eyes double their normal size in a split second?

Sylvester felt that unrelenting pressure on his tail and seemingly said, "I'm out of here!" He flew across the room. There was only one problem— Matthew didn't let go, so he, too, was out of there, laughing all the way. Who was more shocked we'll never know. It was a great laugh for all of us, except the one traumatized family member. My daughter reminded me that a few years later Sylvester went wacko. Who knows why?

Well, did this remembering spark any memories of cat experiences in your life? When did you get your first cat? What was its name? Can you recall the names of all the cats in your life? I remember Marmalade, Boots, Zsa Zsa (she wiggled when she walked), Fluffy, Sylvester, Spunky, Alex, Tuxedo, and Dolly, just to name a few. My brother had a kitten named Tommy that would perch atop a sailor cap on his head as he walked around the yard. The same cat was later renamed Tommie when my brother realized that "he" was a "she."

How have your cats added to your life? What special memories do you have? Take some time to reflect. You'll be amazed at what you remember.

> Wild beasts he created later,
> Lions with their paws so furious,
> In the image of the lion
> Made he kittens small and curious.
> HEINRICH HEINE

CHAPTER TWO
The Cat:
A History of Love & Rejection

I am a cat. Who am I and where did I come from? I have been in hearts and homes for thousands of years. At times I was not only adored, but even worshiped. Those were the best of times for us. But we have also been persecuted. Those were the worst of times.

You can find records of us as far back as 2500 B.C. We began working our way into Egyptian society at this time. Our ancestors were a tabby-like African wild cat. The people appreciated us because we loved to eat their rodents.

Sueellen Ross©

Cats are smarter than dogs. You can't get eight cats to pull a sled through the snow.

JEFF VALDEZ

Around 2000 B.C. there's evidence of the Siamese cat. Far Eastern cultures saw us as omens of good and bad fortune.

In 1500 B.C. we were highly revered. There was a popular cult at this time, called Bast. The populace seemed to think that we personified this goddess of feminine virtue. It sounds good to me. They even established a law that said we couldn't be exported out of the country. So the Greeks kidnapped some of us. I'm sure we inspired many of their great thinkers. In time, they sold us to other countries including Italy. Now some have challenged this. Anthropologists raised the question, "If cats were there, why weren't there any cat bones unearthed at Pompeii?" Simple. We were smart enough not to live next to an active volcano. Just remember, it's not that humans and cats are equal, we're superior.

Guess what? When my Egyptian ancestors died they were actually mummified! Not just a few, but hundreds of thousands. In the nineteenth century archaeologists uncovered 300,000 mummified cats in a dig. The bad news is they shipped them back to England to be used for fertilizer. What a way to end up!

Well, jumping ahead to the eleventh century, the African cats came to Europe and were bred with European wild cats. These were not good times for us. We were persecuted by the Christian church because of our association with pagan cults. It wasn't our fault for this connection.

It wasn't much different in the thirteenth century. Crusaders brought cats from Eastern Europe. People started to like us again because they used us to kill rats. But then the cults began to revive and people believed we were direct agents of the devil, ruining our reputation.

Most cats, when they are Out
want to be In, and vice versa,
and often simultaneously.

BARBARA HOLLAND

Sueellen Ross

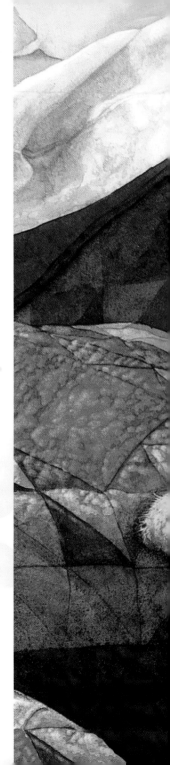

More centuries went by, and we began to spread all over the world. Wherever men went on their ships, we went. When they went ashore, so did we. And some of us stayed. By the eighteenth century many of us had beautiful long hair. The royalty of Europe loved the Angoras and Persians, and they should. We are very intelligent. Who else can say it all with one word, "Meow?"

And guess what happened in the nineteenth century? Cat shows were started in Britain. We not only survived, but we arrived. Just look at the past hundred years:

In 1919 *Felix the Cat* made his debut in films. I'm sure you've heard of *Puss'n'Boots* cat food (it smells so good). It was one of the first nationally marketed cat foods in 1934. And 1945 was the year for Sylvester to emerge in cartoons.

Do you know when the first issue of *Cat Fancy* magazine was published? 1965.

Who doesn't know Morris? His commercials were released in 1969, and in 1975 he proclaimed June adopt-a-cat month!

1985 was a very good year. That's the year we cats overtook dogs as the most numerous animal companion in the United States. We still are! Thirty-four percent of all households own a cat. Yes, we're here to stay.

Come, lovely cat, and rest upon my heart,

And let my gaze dive in the cold

Live pools of thine enchanted eyes that dart

Metallic rays of green and gold.

CHARLES BAUDELAIR

Sueellen Ross

CHAPTER THREE

Feline Fun

Cats are so much a part of our everyday lives. Just look how they have worked their way into our vocabulary! Check out the following phrases and see if you can "cat"ch the meaning:

1. A short rest period is a…
2. A child's game played with a piece of string…
3. The runway used by fashion models is a…
4. A thief who dresses in all black…
5. When you can't seem to find the words because the…
6. A person who appears suspiciously guilty looks like…
7. When something is super cool, you say it's the…
8. The game when you toy with something by releasing and capturing it…
9. In the hospital, you get your head X-rayed in a…
10. Long brown furry reeds that grow along the edge of a pond are…
11. A special type of marble…
12. A strong-smelling herb felines go crazy for…
13. A deep-fried Southern delicacy…
14. A serious devotee of jazz music…
15. When you're in a place of prominence, you're sitting in the…

(You'll find the answers on page 2.)

Way down deep, we're all

motivated by the same urges.

Cats have the courage

to live by them.

JIM DAVIS

SueEllen Ross

CHAPTER FOUR
Escapades of a Kitten

My name is Mozart. I just turned three. Three months, that is. And I'm special. I'm a British Shorthair. And no! I do not meow with a British accent.

The person I own wakes me up at 6:00 A.M. and am I ready for the day! I love to play. Let me describe my morning for you. There's just so much to explore once I hit the kitchen. Every nook and cranny has to be climbed and explored, even the kitchen table. Unfortunately, the people here don't appreciate my agility. They're so territorial! You would think they would cut me some slack because I cleanse their precious kitchen from every bug I see (and some that exist only in my mind). This morning I caught a fly, a moth, two spiders, and one earwig. Yum! I look in every open cupboard, and I consider every open door an invitation to explore. I just love boxes and vases that can be tipped over.

SueellenRoss

Cats seem to go on the principle that it never does any harm to ask for what you want.

JOSEPH WOOD KRUTCH

Sueellen Ross

Sometimes I get running so fast, when I go to stop my feet, I skid and slide right past that toy I'm playing with. Why do humans always laugh at me? I don't think it's so funny.

The other morning I snuck into another room and guess what I found? A snake! Yes, I did. It was thrashing up and down, and it was also furry. So, I thought it was my job to destroy it. I jumped on it and sank my claws in, but it lifted me off the floor. Help! It wasn't a snake after all. It was the tail of an 80-pound Golden Retriever. He wasn't very amused. I bet he never saw a kitten run so fast in his life.

Well, enough is enough. I've played, explored, created chaos in my wake, and received a few "get out of there" comments. Now I'm off to eat and sleep. Later on, I'll repeat the whole process again and again and again. I just love being a kitten!

CHAPTER FIVE

What Do You Really Know About Your Cat?

I've owned cats for more than 50 years (yes, regardless of what a cat believes, I still think I'm the owner). Perhaps you have a longer history, or you might just be starting out. Even though you and I have had many cats, we really don't understand what they're doing or why they're doing what they're doing. And it could be such simple things. Consider, for example, these basic questions.

Why does your cat purr?

Why does your cat wag its tail?

What do cats think about doors?

Can cats predict earthquakes?

I know you haven't lost any sleep dwelling upon these profound and life-changing questions, but just stop for a moment. How would you answer each of these? You hear your cat purr. You see the tail wagging. And your cat wants the door to open to go outside and immediately wants it open again to come inside. Why?

We cannot, without becoming cats,

perfectly understand the cat mind.

ST. GEORGE MIVART

Sueellen Ross

Some believe a purring cat is a content cat. But cats purr during pain and in labor. They're not really content during these times. Contentment is just one reason for purring. Most often, it signals a friendly social mood. A mother cat purrs as her kittens feed, letting them know she is in a relaxed mood. Her kittens begin purring at one week-old while feeding, and their purr lets their mother know all is well.

Dogs wag their tails. They're supposed to. It's a form of communication. Well, so is the wagging of a cat's tail. It's true it can indicate anger. Most of the time it signals a state of conflict. You know what it's like when you want to do two things at once, but each impulse blocks the other. That's what's going on with your cat. It's not really anger. Your cat isn't in an aggressive state. It's sort of stuck. When your cat is pulled in two directions at once, it stops and wags its tail. When it's resolved, the tail stops.

What do cats think about doors? It's simple. They hate them. They're unnecessary. They stymie a cat from its natural patrolling activities. When a cat wants to be let out, it has a purpose. It wants to survey its territory and get an update on what all the other cats are doing. Your cat doesn't want or need to stay outside very long, so you have to get up, open the door again, and let her in. You may not like opening and closing the door so much, but your cat dislikes it even more. She wants to come and go at will. You know, to be in control! She has to be dependent upon you, and no cat wants to have to depend upon a human. If you don't believe me, just ask them.

I have lived in earthquake country for more than 60 years. I've been through some major ones over the years. Each came as a surprise. There was no warning. No one could predict them. I wish we could have. But what about cats? Can they predict

earthquakes? It's true, they can. We're not sure how. It could be they're sensitive to the earth's vibrations or the increase in static electricity that precedes earthquakes. Or perhaps they're responsive to sudden shifts in the earth's magnetic fields.

Whatever the reason, many cats have become very agitated just before major earthquakes. Some have rushed around trying to escape from the house. Some mother cats will rush back and forth carrying her kittens to safety. The same behavior has been noted on the part of cats just before volcanic eruptions or severe electrical storms. Perhaps someday we will understand why and be able to make better use of our cats' built-in early warning system.

SueEllen Ross©

Cats have a contempt of speech. Why should they talk when they can communicate without words?

Lilian Jackson Braun

CHAPTER SIX

"I'm Smart, If Not Brilliant"

"**Sylvester** is my name and brains are my game. Can you imagine? Someone had the *audacity* (that's a cat word—you won't find a dog using it) to raise the question, do cats think? Of course we think. We all do. Sure, some of us are very smart and a few come from the shallow end of the brain gene pool, but we're all intelligent. The Siamese claim they're the smartest, but they're just delusional.

"Our smarts come out in many ways. We are cautious. There are other animals that aren't smart enough to know there's danger. We'll even explore things we don't need to explore—just to see what they are!

Dogs come when they're called. Cats take a message and get back to you.

MARY BLY

SueEllen Ross

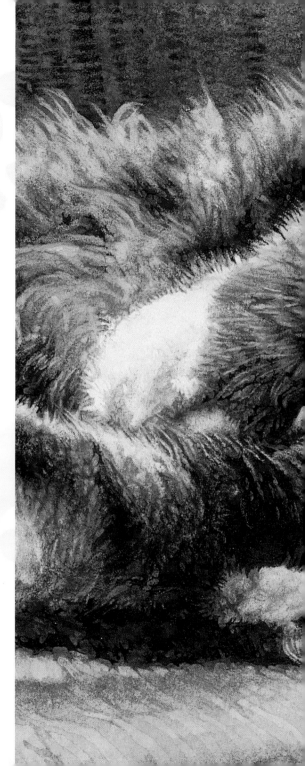

"We have the ability to solve problems and adapt. We are independent-minded and have wills of our own. Don't try to teach us to press buttons or pull strings to get food. We'll just fall asleep.

"We can learn. I learned about the litter box from my mother. Just from watching her. Do you have any idea of how much I can learn? Well, here it goes. I can learn (if I decide to cooperate) to sit, beg, eat with my paws, jump through a hoop, play a piano, play dead, roll over, shake, and fetch—just to mention a few. I won't learn by your voice, but by your rewards. You know—food and goodies.

"Can we remember? Much more than you think—especially if it's useful. People think they train us. It's the other way around. We remember which noises to use to get the person we own to do what we want!"

There are people who reshape the world by force or argument, but the cat just lies there, dozing, and the world quietly reshapes itself to suit his comfort and convenience.

ALLEN AND IVY DODD

Sueellen Ross

CHAPTER SEVEN

Cats-
How Many Breeds?

Sueellen Ross

It's amazing—there are many ways to classify cats. How would you describe your feline? Do you know its breed? Body type?

Breeds come and go. In the past few decades we have seen the creation of several new ones with probably more to come.

Consider the American Bobtail. No one is quite certain how it originated. It has a short tail from one to six inches long. It's playful, patient, and can master tricks. It speaks in chirps and trills more than meows.

Some breeds have died out and some are not recognized by different cat organizations. Today there are about 100 pedigree breeds that are recognized (not by all cat associations) and fall into these four categories: Longhair, Siamese, Shorthair, and Foreign Shorthair. The most popular breed is Persians—if measured by the number entered into cat shows.

We have pedigree cats and tabby cats. The latter is what most of us have, a non-pedigree (and affordable) cat. They are sometimes grouped according to body type.

There's the Cobby type—compact body, deep chest, short legs, broad head, and large round eyes. The Muscular type has a sturdy body and a round, full-cheeked head. Foreign types have a slender body with a long tail and legs. The head is different—it's wedge-shaped with tall ears and slanting eyes.

I wonder what cats say about us? Knowing them, I'm sure they have an opinion!

CHAPTER EIGHT

Did You Know?

Cats are basically nocturnal animals. They sleep about 16 hours a day. Translated, this means a 7-year-old cat has been awake for just about 2 years of its life, or a 14-year-old cat has been awake just about 4 years of its life.

With cats, color does have an effect upon their gender. Calico cats are always female.

What does it cost you at the vet to own a cat? The average is about 80 dollars per year for the life of your cat.

Cats came into their own when the first cat show was held in this country. Where? Madison Square Garden in New York in 1895.

How much time do you spend bathing? The average person spends a year-and-a-half of their life grooming. Whatever it is, it won't come close to a cat's participation in this activity. Would you believe they spend 30 percent of their waking hours grooming themselves?

There is, indeed,
no single quality of
cat that man could
not emulate to
his advantage.
CARL VAN VECHTEN

Sueellen Ross

❧ Are you left-handed, right-handed, or ambidextrous? What about your cat? About 40 percent of them are ambidextrous, another 40 percent are right-pawed, and the others are left-pawed.

❧ Are cats going to take over the world? Probably not, but there are lots of them. More than 500 million domestic cats live on this planet. Approximately 65 to 70 million of those live in the United States.

❧ Everyone seems to be living longer nowadays. Since the 1930s the average life expectancy of cats has nearly doubled—from eight years to 16. And the oldest cat in modern times lived to be 36!

❧ The names have changed. Goodbye, Felix and Josephine. The most popular names now are Tiger and Samantha.

❧ Have you ever watched your cat walk? Well, your feline friend walks just like a camel or giraffe. In fact, these are the only three in the animal kingdom with a gait in which front and hind legs move together, first on one side, then on the other.

❧ What color are your cat's eyes? No matter what they are now they were blue at birth. That's true for all cats.

❧ Have you ever seen your cat's eyes glow at night? That's called "night shine." It's actually a reflection from a mirror in the

cat's retina. It produces a fluorescent quality and occurs when a sudden blaze of light hits the wide-open pupils that have been in the dark. They don't see well in the darkness, but they see better than we can.

❧ Cats can go up those trees so fast and with such ease, it's amazing. But coming down is another matter and for good reason. Their claws point in one direction— forward—so climbing is great. Coming back down just doesn't work so well.

❧ Have you ever wondered what your cat can see? Imagine yourself looking through frosted glass or a window that's steamed up a bit. Details aren't too sharp for them, although their peripheral vision is better than ours. And they can see colors, but they probably see things in more gray and green tones.

 Cats are agile. They can't fly nor do they have a built-in parachute, yet somehow they have the ability to survive falls from heights that would do us in. Not only that, they do better on longer falls than shorter. Probably because it gives them more time to spread their bodies like parachutes so they can land correctly. In Portland, Oregon, a pregnant cat was accidentally knocked off a bridge. She not only survived, but a few days later gave birth to a healthy litter of kittens.

 And, yes, it's true, cats almost always land on their feet.

Sueellen Ross

CHAPTER NINE

House Cat Heroics

Cats have saved people in many ways. They have alerted their sleeping owners when there has been a fire. Sometimes they cry, lick their owner's nose, or paw at them. They have also warned their owners by jumping on them and mewing when there was a gas leak.

One of the strangest rescues was by a small Abyssinian by the name of Trixy. Her 79-year-old owner fell in front of his home and broke his hip. He was unable to move and no one could hear him—except Trixy. She began to paw nervously around her master and then noticed a dinner bell that was hung outside the house. The only

It is as easy to hold
quicksilver between
your finger and thumb
as to keep a cat who
means to escape.
ANDREW LANG

SueellenRoss

problem was her owner had recently tied the bell up so Trixy couldn't get to it and bother the neighbors.

Trixy had given up on the bell until now. She leaped three feet in the air, snared the rope with her teeth, and hung on for dear life. She swung from side to side, ringing the bell, and then fell. She got up, grabbed the rope, and rang the bell again and again. In time, the neighbors came over to see what was wrong and found the injured man. Soon the ambulance arrived, and while her owner recuperated, Trixy was well cared for by others.

Sometimes a cat's efforts are not what they seem to be. In Troy, New York, the police received a 911 call from someone who sounded hurt and almost too weak to speak. All they could hear were two words—Me...ow. The police arrived at the home and when no one responded to the knock on the apartment door, they broke

in through a screened window. All they found was Yeager, who had apparently pawed the pad of a programmed push-button phone and dialed 911. What the 911 operator heard was "Meow" not "me..ow." The officers left a note saying, "Your cat called the police, we had to break in." No charges were brought against Yeager for filing a false report.

Many homes today have alarm systems. Some have a sign in front of their home stating this fact and warning about an armed response. Well, a burglar in San Diego, California, would have benefited by such a sign before he entered a home with a guard cat named Jake.

The intruder entered the home around 2:00 A.M., put his hand over the occupant's mouth, a young woman, and told her not to make a sound. That was the wrong thing to do and say. All of a sudden Jake, a 21-year-old feline (a real senior citizen), went into action. He jumped the intruder and scratched and clawed him so much, the man fled. Later he was caught and identified as the woman's neighbor. They didn't need a lineup to single him out, either. The scratches all over his arms and shoulders were all the evidence they needed, thanks to Jake.

J.B. was a big orange and white tabby. Karen adopted him from a shelter  and said he was everything she didn't want in a cat. He had lived in the wild for a while and his paws were rough and badly cut. A week after he was adopted, Karen was awakened by J.B. scratching her neck with his claws. She fell back to sleep but was awakened once again by his claws digging into her neck. This time he woke her up. The next thing she heard was someone removing the screen from her window. She called 911 and in a couple of minutes heard the sirens. That sound scared off the would-be intruders. J.B. knew something was wrong and took direct action. It wasn't just something that happened by chance. He never scratched Karen again.

Hear our prayer, Lord,
for all animals.
May they be well-fed
and well-trained and happy;
Protect them from hunger
and fear and suffering,
And, we pray, protect
especially, dear Lord,
The little cat who is the
companion of our home,
Keep her safe as she goes abroad,
And bring her back to comfort us.

ANONYMOUS

CHAPTER TEN

Natural Navigators

Story after story has been documented about traveling cats. A family was moving from Pennsylvania to Minnesota. Before they arrived at their destination, their 12-year-old cat escaped from its cage in Illinois. They searched for hours but never found Satin. Months later a neighbor from Pennsylvania called to tell them their cat had arrived back home. The cat made the 800-mile journey in about 11 months. How could a cat do this?

How do they do it? How do these cats find their way home? Did you know that cats have a built-in navigation system similar to that used by birds?

SueellenRoss

When a cat lives in the same house for a while, its brain automatically registers the angle of the sun at certain times of the day. When a cat is taken away from its residence, it can find that house again by using its internal biological clock and, through trial and error, it puts

the sun back in the right place again. Not only that, a cat doesn't have to have a clear, sun-filled day. It uses polarized light.

And that's not all. Somehow a cat has sensitivity to the earth's magnetic fields. If you want to disrupt a cat's navigational skills, just attach a magnet to him. That will do it. That's how they remember where they live.

But how do you explain the accounts of cats left behind only to show up at their owner's new residence?

Clementine was left behind in New York when her owner moved to Denver.

Yet three months later, her coat matted, paws cracked and worn, her tail resembling an old rag, Clementine showed up at her owner's new home.

Tom holds the record for traveling—2,500 miles. His owners left him in San Gabriel, California, when they moved to Florida. But two years and six months later, he showed up at his owner's new home in Florida. How do cats accomplish this? How would you explain this ability? Perhaps we weren't meant to know. It's one of the many mysteries of a cat.

> There are people who reshape the world by force or argument, but the cat just lies there, dozing, and the world quietly reshapes itself to suit his comfort and convenience
>
> ALLEN DODD

CHAPTER ELEVEN

Therapy Cats

Therapy appears to be the "in" word now. It seems that nearly everyone is involved in some form of therapy. Most of us have heard of "therapy dogs"—the seeing-eye dog, guide dogs for the hearing impaired, canine companion dogs for the disabled. Have you ever seen a "seeing-eye cat"? Not likely, and you probably won't. But cats can become a "pet partner" or therapy cat.

A special bond can exist between cats and people. Many of our needs are filled by our cats. We have a need to nurture that is often a void in the lives of many, especially those who are disabled or elderly. A cat gives us something to take care of which fulfills our need to be needed.

Cats provide us with entertainment. They give us enjoyment and hours of laughter. Have you ever watched

There are no ordinary cats.

COLETTE

Sueellen Ross

a group of seniors in a retirement home sitting around watching and laughing over the antics of two kittens tearing around? You'll hear laughter and see smiles. You'll hear them saying, "I remember our cat. . ." and "When I was a little girl. . ." Happy memories come rushing back. These times provide a delightful relief from the day-to-day routine.

Cats are being used more and more to help overcome loneliness and depression, encourage activity, improve self-confidence, and reduce anxiety and blood pressure. They've even helped people who are grieving the loss of a loved one.

Cats are often used in convalescent centers, nursing homes, senior homes, assisted living centers, and veterans' hospitals. Some come to visit while others have taken up residency. Cats have been especially helpful for those suffering dementia or Alzheimer's to activate memories.

Buster, Flashback, and Flame are three cats that have touched the lives of hundreds. They've been taught to come running when they hear car keys jangling, ride in the car, walk on a leash, and give their paw in greeting. Their owner takes them to visit public libraries and shelters for abandoned children. They are used to teach children to love, understand, and take responsibility for animals. They also make visits to the Miami Children's Hospital, nursing homes, and various educational institutions. As one elderly resident said, "Oh, it's like therapy when they come to visit. I feel good all over and that feeling stays with me the rest of the day. I love it when they come because they lay on your lap and love you."

So many people are starving for touch and love. Cats can help fill that need.

The ideal of calm exists in a sitting cat.

Jules Reynard

Sueellen Ross

CHAPTER TWELVE

Whiskers— Ornamental or Useful?

Some owners like to trim their cat's whiskers. Don't! They're not for show. They have a purpose—in fact, they have several purposes:

🐾 Cats use their whiskers to determine if their prey is dead. Have you ever watched a cat with a mouse in its mouth? He may touch it with his whiskers to see if it's moving. If it isn't, it's probably safe to put the mouse down without it running away.

🐾 A cat doesn't have to see a mouse. It can sense a mouse from air currents on its whiskers.

🐾 Did you know that cats are farsighted? They rely upon their whiskers to help them "see" better when objects are close and out of focus.

🐾 Cats' whiskers are wider than their body, so it's possible to use them like feelers to see if they'll be able to fit through narrow places.

If a dog jumps in your lap, it's because he's fond of you; but if a cat does the same thing, it is because your lap is warmer.

ALFRED NORTH WHITEHEAD

Sweellen Ross

CHAPTER THIRTEEN

The Little Marine

Tony, my cat, was five years old when I found him at the Denver Dumb Friends League. Five years later, I had major surgery that kept me homebound for several months. A trip from the bedroom to the living room took a half hour—on a good day.

Overnight, Tony changed from a pet to a guardian with canine actions. He was by my side constantly—literally my shadow.

When I was in the living room, he was on the ottoman—eyes at half-mast, never ever closed.

When I was in the bedroom, he was at the foot of the bed, ever alert.

When I was in the shower, he was sitting beside the tub.

When I was in the kitchen, he was in the doorway.

The only time he truly slept was when my mother or friends he trusted were over to make meals—or when I was asleep.

Sueellen Ross

If I was in the living room or kitchen and he needed some solid sleep, he would curl around the legs of my walker, because he knew I couldn't go anywhere without using it—thus waking him.

If we were in the bedroom and someone came in the unlocked front door, he would bound off the bed and be in full attack mode—until he saw who the intruder was.

Overnight, he transformed himself from a happy-go-lucky critter into a guard who took his very job seriously.

We called him The Little Marine.

Though still friendly, he would not leave my side to solicit attention from visitors—something he used to run to people for.

If they wanted to pet him, they had to come by me and I had to give them permission to pet him.

He used to love to play; however, he knew that I simply couldn't, so he never solicited it.

That was almost two years ago. To this day, I marvel at the transformation this wonderful creature made to care for me in my months of need. When things seem difficult now, I think of how my little Marine summoned the strength to support me, and things seem easier. He is an inspiration to everyone who knows him.

Although I once thought this would be impossible, his devotion has deepened our bond immeasurably. I now love watching him curl up and fall sound asleep, not a care in the world—or bounce over to company and throw himself on their feet so they have to pet him. I deny him almost nothing today. He gave up months of his life to selflessly serve and protect me, so the least I can do is play ball for half an hour in the evening or join him on the balcony on balmy days and quietly watch this noble critter have a well-deserved rest.

–JUDY DRAGO

Sueellen Ross

CHAPTER FOURTEEN

Sacrificial Sharing Makes Best Friends

A Virginia veterinarian told the tearful owners of Smoke, an ailing gray and white cat, "His kidneys are failing." The childless couple enjoyed a special love for this cat, who was a stray they had found and adopted. They asked the vet a strange question to most, "Was there any possibility of a kidney transplant?" The vet was hesitant but said, "We could look into it, I suppose." Smoke's owners surfed the Internet that night and located several specialists who performed the operation. They chose the nearest clinic, which was 450 miles away in Buffalo.

There is no more intrepid explorer than a kitten.

Jules Champfleury

Sueellen Ross

The Buffalo veterinarian agreed to begin to search for a kidney match, but with one stipulation—the donor had to be selected from the Prevention of Cruelty to Animals (S.P.C.A.) shelter. Two-thirds of the cats there were put to sleep because no one adopted them. He also had a second condition: "After  the transplant, you have to adopt the donor cat." His r e q u i r e m e n t would save two lives—the cat that would otherwise be euthanized and the cat that would die of kidney failure. The couple agreed.

After a four-and-a-half-hour surgery, it was over. A kidney slightly smaller than a plum was removed from a buff-colored kitten donor and transplanted into Smoke. They both survived. Two days later, Buffalo, the newly named kitten, went to his new home. Three weeks later, Smoke was ready to return home and to meet Buffalo, the best friend of his life. Today the two cats are great buddies and will surely be friends fur-ever.

A cat knows how to be comfortable, how to get the people around it to serve it. In a tranquil domestic situation, the cat is a veritable manipulative genius. It seeks the soft, it seeks the warm, it prefers the quiet and it loves to be full...If we could relax like a cat we would probably live at least 125 years, and then we could relax to death. Cats know how NOT to get ulcers. We may seek that level of tranquility, but we seldom achieve it.

ROGER CARAS

Recommended Books on Cats

277 Secrets Your Cat Wants You to Know by Paulette Cooper and Paul Noble (Ten Speed Press, 1997)

Cat Facts by Marcus Schneck and Jill Caravan (A Quantum Book, 1990)

Cats Incredible! by Brad Steiger (A Plume Book, 1994)

CatWatching by Desmond Morris (Random House Publishers, 1986)

Fun Facts About Cats—Inspiring Tales, Amazing Feats, and Helpful Hints by Richard Torregrossa (Health Communications, 1998)

Puss in Boots edited by Maria Plushkin Robbins (The Ecco Press, 1994)

The Cats of Our Lives edited by Franklin Dohanyos (Carol Publishing Group, 1999)

Think Like a Cat: How to Raise a Well-Adjusted Cat—Not a Sour Puss by Pam Johnson Bennet (Penguin Books, 2000)

What My Cat Has Taught Me About Life by Niki Anderson (Honor Books, 1997)

Acknowledgments

"How Cats Enrich Our Lives" is adapted from *The Joy of Cats* by Jo Kitlinger (New York: Meadowbrook Press, 1999).

"What Do You Really Know About Your Cat" is adapted from *Catwatching* by Desmond Morris (New York: Crown, 1986), pp. 17-18; 39-40; 50-51; 126-127.

"I'm Smart, If Not Brilliant" is adapted from *Cat Facts* by Marcus Schneck and Jill Caravan (London: Quantum Books, 1990), pp. 18-21.

"Cats—How Many Breeds?" is adapted from *Cat Facts* by Marcus Schneck and Jill Caravan (London: Quantum Books, 1990), pp. 10-11.

"House Cat Heroics" is adapted from *Cats Incredible* by Brad Steiger (New York: Plume Books, 1994) pp. 15-16; 152-153.

"House Cat Heroics" is also adapted from the July/August 1999 *Pets, Part of the Family*, p. 68.

"Natural Navigators" is adapted from *Cat Facts* by Marcus Schneck and Jill Caravan (London: Quantum Books, 1990), p. 21.

"Therapy Cats" is adapted from *Delta Society Stories*, Renton, WA.

"Whiskers—Ornamental or Useful?" is adapted from *277 Secrets Your Cat Wants You to Know* by Paulette Cooper and Paul Noble (Berkeley: Ten Speed Press, 1997), p. 178.

"The Little Marine" is adapted from *Cat Caught My Heart* by Michael Zapuzzo and Teresa Banick Zapuzzo (New York: Bantam Books, 1998), pp. 70-72.

"Sacrificial Sharing Makes Best Friends" is adapted from *What My Cat Has Taught Me About Life* by Niki Anderson (Tulsa, OK: Honor Books, 1977), pp. 114-115.